Brazil

Elizabeth Weitzman

ℵ Carolrhoda Books, Inc. / Minneapolis

Photo Acknowledgments

Photographs, maps, and artworks are used courtesy of: John Erste, pp. 1, 2–3, 9, 11, 21, 25, 27, 30–31, 37, 39, 41; Laura Westlund, pp. 4, 15; © SuperStock, Inc., pp. 6 (left), 10 (left); © Michele Burgess, pp. 6–7, 8, 24 (left); D. Donne Bryant Stock: (© Juca Martins) pp. 7, 19 (right), (© Craig Duncan) p. 9 (top), (© Nair Benedicto) pp. 9 (bottom), 11, 13, 25, 40, (© Stefan Kolumban) p. 16, (© Robert Fried) pp. 18, 26, (© Michael Moody) p. 19 (left), (© Ricardo Teles) p. 27, (© Mauricio Simonetti) pp. 29, 34, (© Vince DeWitt) p. 35 (top); Visuals Unlimited: (© Erwin C. "Bud" Nielsen) p. 10 (bottom right), (© Beth Davidow) p.22 (right); © Buddy Mays/TRAVEL STOCK, pp. 10 (top right); © Sue Cunningham/SCP, pp. 12, 23 (bottom), 31, 36, 37 (both), 38, 42, 43 (both); © Wolfgang Kaehler, pp. 14, 22 (left), 33 (left), 45; © Mary Altier, pp. 15 (bottom), 21, 41; TOM STACK & ASSOCIATES: (© Byron Augustin) pp. 15 (top), 32; TRIP: (© M. Barlow) pp. 17, 23 (top), (© R. Belbin) p. 24 (right), (© D. Harding) p. 28, (© S. Grant) p. 33 (right), (© Eric Smith) p. 44; © Bettmann, p. 35 (bottom). Cover photo © Manfred Gottschalk, TOM STACK & ASSOCIATES.

Carolrhoda Books, Inc.
c/o The Lerner Publishing Group
241 First Avenue North
Minneapolis, Minnesota 55401 U.S.A.

Website address: www.lernerbooks.com

Words in **bold type** are explained in a glossary that begins on p. 44.

Library of Congress Cataloging-in-Publication Data

Weitzman, Elizabeth.
    Brazil / by Elizabeth Weitzman.
        p.   cm. — (Globe-trotters club)
    Includes index.
    Summary: An overview of Brazil, emphasizing its cultural aspects.
    ISBN 1–57505–107–9 (lib. bdg.: alk. paper)
    1. Brazil—Juvenile literature. [1. Brazil.] I. Title.
    II. Series: Globe-trotters club (Series)
F2508.5.W45   1998
981—DC21   97–18773

Manufactured in the United States of America
1 2 3 4 5 6 – JR – 03 02 01 00 99 98

Contents

Benvindos ao
Brasil!*

That's "Welcome to Brazil" in Portuguese, the official language of Brazil.

In 1500 Pedro Alvares Cabral landed on the eastern shores of South America. He was a little confused. Cabral and his crew had left Portugal looking for the continent of Asia. Well, they should have returned their maps for a refund. Asia is all the way across the globe from South America!

Although Cabral missed his goal by thousands of miles, he made a pretty cool discovery. He found himself on the coast of what is now one of the biggest countries in the world—Brazil. This huge land takes up almost half of the continent of South America. The eastern edge of Brazil stretches along the Atlantic Ocean and has the longest coastline on earth. Brazil's other borders touch every other nation on the continent except Ecuador and Chile. Altogether Brazil has 26 states and one federal district.

Brazil has some of the most beautiful and exotic plants and animals that humans have ever seen. Many of them live in the Amazon forest in northern Brazil. This lush **tropical rain forest** spreads out to eight other countries in South America. Thousands of different kinds of trees grow in the Amazon. So it's fitting that Brazil is named after one of them—the brazilwood tree.

Q. Pedro Cabral wasn't the only European to set off for Asia and find himself in the Americas instead. Can you name another explorer who could have used a better mapmaker?

A. (Christopher Columbus)

5

Are We Still in
Brazil?

 If you visited every corner of Brazil, you'd see a lot of different landscapes. The Amazon region in the north contains the powerful Amazon River and the huge Amazon rain forest. This region is so big it covers more than half of Brazil.

Coconut trees grow along the Coastal Plain. This strip of flat land stretches along the Atlantic coast in northeastern Brazil. Farmers raise cocoa beans and sugarcane in the rich soil. Big cities such as Recife and Salvador are in this region, too.

Farther inland is the *sertão*, or backlands. **Droughts** strike this dry, hilly area. One of Brazil's biggest rivers—the São Francisco— flows across the sertão. But watch your step! Cactuses and prickly shrubs grow here.

The São Francisco River is more than 1,000 miles long.

From the hustle and bustle of São Paulo (far left) **to the beauty of Iguaçu Falls** (left), **Brazil offers a variety of landscapes.**

Brazil's biggest cities, Rio de Janeiro and São Paulo, lie along the Atlantic coast in southern Brazil. Cattle roam and huge coffee plantations (farms) go on for miles in the pampas (grasslands) of southern Brazil. Also in the south are the Iguaçu Falls. This incredible group of 275 waterfalls spreads across two miles and pounds into the Iguaçu River with a thundering roar. The gorgeous falls send dozens of rainbows into the air with their water sprays.

Southwestern Brazil is home to the Pantanal. At least 2,000 kinds of animals live in this huge, swampy region. If you went there, you could find alligators, boa constrictors, otters, and jabiru birds. Jabirus, a type of stork, can grow as big as the tallest person in your class!

A jabiru bird

7

Did you know that Brazil has some of the world's most famous beaches?

How's the
Weather?

Winter in Brazil starts in June and ends in August. But if you visit then, leave your mittens at home! In most areas of Brazil, the temperature hardly ever drops below 65°F. In the summer, which lasts from December to March, it can get *really* hot. People in some parts of the country aren't surprised if the temperature tops 107°F. It's a good thing Brazil has all those beaches.

Just when you pull on your hats and scarves, Brazilian kids get out their bathing suits. Why? Well, you've heard of the **equator,** that line that goes around the center of a globe? The equator divides the world into the **Northern Hemisphere** (above the equator) and the **Southern Hemisphere** (below the equator). The United States is north of the equator. Because Brazil lies south of the equator, its seasons are the exact opposite of ours.

During Brazil's hot summers, kids on the coast stay cool by swimming in the Atlantic Ocean.

8

Large amounts of rain keep the Amazon region (above) **lush and green, but lack of rain in central Brazil often leads to drought** (left).

Fast Facts about Brazil

Name: República Federativa do Brasil (Federative Republic of Brazil)

Area: 3.3 million square miles

Main Landforms: Amazon River, Pantanal, Iguaçu Falls, São Francisco River, Guiana Highlands, Brazilian Highlands

Highest Point: Pico da Neblina (9,888 feet)

Lowest Point: Sea level

Animals: Parrots, macaws, jaguars, alligators, sloths, armadillos, monkeys, anteaters, electric eels, and too many more to list!

Capital City: Brasília

Other Major Cities: Rio de Janeiro, São Paulo, Recife, Salvador, Pôrto Alegre

Official Language: Portuguese

Money Unit: Real

Snow doesn't fall in too many places in Brazil. But when it rains, it pours. The Amazon region gets more than 160 inches of rain each year. That's enough to fill a bucket that's almost 14 feet high—higher than the ceilings in your home! On the other hand, central Brazil hardly gets any rain at all. Droughts may last as long as two years.

The Amazon River is the chief river of South America. At some points, it is more than six miles wide!

A toucan (above) and a squirrel monkey (below)

Good News... and
Bad News

Brazilians are proud of the lush Amazon rain forest and the mighty Amazon River. The river is the second longest in the world, and the **river basin** contains about one-quarter of the planet's fresh water. Thousands of animals live here. There are anteaters and monkeys, electric eels and sharp-toothed piranhas, macaws, and toucans. There are more insects than you'd ever want to see, including 200 types of mosquitoes! In one square mile, you might find 3,000 different kinds of trees.

But the Amazon rain forest is in trouble. Mining, farming, and logging companies want to use the land. They are cutting down trees, burning the forest, and polluting the waters. This doesn't only hurt the animals and plants in the Amazon. It also hurts us. For example, medicines made from plants that grow in the Amazon may help cure cancer and other diseases. But when a living **species** is gone, it's gone forever. One less type of plant is one less possible cure.

Some Amazonian trees can grow 165 feet into the sky—that's as tall as a 20-story building.

To clear land for farming, many Brazilian farmers have burned down parts of the rain forest. This practice threatens the future of the Amazon region.

The First **Brazilians**

Although some early Portuguese settlers learned the customs and languages of Brazil's native peoples, many forced the Indians into slavery. Enslaving Indians became illegal in 1570.

 Millions of native peoples (or Indians) lived in Brazil when Portuguese explorers first landed in 1500. Hundreds of years later, only about 200,000 Indians remain.

Before the Portuguese came, there were no outsiders to interfere with the native peoples' way of life (although they sometimes fought one another). Almost as soon as Portuguese settlers arrived, they began forcing Indians to work as slaves on plantations and in gold mines. Many of the Indians died from sickness and overwork. Other Indians escaped deep into the Amazon.

In recent years, Brazil's government has forced some Indians to move off their land and into cities. But many of these Indians don't have skills for city jobs. They have trouble finding work, so they are very poor.

Other Indians in Brazil continue to live in large tribes far from cities. The Yanomami are probably the largest Indian group that hasn't moved into the cities. They live in the Amazon rain forest. Like their ancestors, they hunt for food and fight with bows and arrows. Following ancient customs, another Amazon group called the Txucarramae stretch out their lower lips with wood plates. They also cover their bodies with tribal markings during special ceremonies.

The Kaiapo Indians of the Amazon region have tried to preserve their culture and traditional way of life.

Factoid

More than 300 different Indian nations once lived in Brazil. Only about 200 groups remain. Deep in the Amazon rain forest, there may be more Indian peoples who live without any contact with the modern world.

A Blend of
Cultures

More than 160 million people live in Brazil. They come from all kinds of backgrounds—native, European, African, and Asian. Lots of Brazilians have ancestors from different cultures. That's because it's very common in Brazil for people of different backgrounds to marry one another. *Caboclos* have a combination of European and Indian ancestors. *Cafusos* can trace their roots to African and Indian parents and grandparents. Mulattoes have European and African ancestors.

In the 1500s, the Portuguese brought black people from Africa to replace Indian slaves in Brazil. Slavery became illegal in Brazil in 1888. Many blacks then settled in the state of Bahia, in northeastern Brazil. African culture is probably strongest in Salvador, Bahia's capital. But African influences are found all over Brazil. Food, music, religion, and dance are just some of the areas that have borrowed from African Brazilian culture.

This group of Brazilian schoolgirls represents the variety of ethnic backgrounds in Brazil.

No Touching Allowed!

African slaves in Brazil were punished for fighting, so they came up with a fighting style that looked like dancing. Over the years, *capoeira* has become a unique sport that combines dancing and the defensive skills of the **martial arts**. Capoeiras try to move without touching one another at all. And they have to do it while spinning and kicking to the rhythm of drums and a one-stringed instrument called a *berimbau*.

Dear Grandma and Grandpa:
Yesterday we arrived in Salvador, the capital of Bahia. It's beautiful here! The streets are steep and curvy, and all the houses are painted different colors, like pink, green, and yellow. Many of the people here are African Brazilians. Some of the women, who are called Bahianas, wear African-style clothes. They wrap pretty scarves high on their heads and wear lace blouses and long, full skirts. Mom bought me some wooden beads like the ones the Bahianas wear. I'll write more later—it's time for lunch! Everyone says we have to try *acarajé*, fried bean cakes stuffed with shrimp and peppers.
Tchau!
(That's "See ya later" in Portuguese.)

A Land of
Contrasts

Like most giant countries, Brazil is a land of contrasts. Big cities such as Rio de Janeiro and São Paulo have very, very rich people and really, really poor people. The wealthy people often have chauffeurs to drive their cars, cooks to prepare their meals, and maids to do the housework. The adults have good jobs, and their kids go to private schools.

But only a few miles away are slums called favelas. Homes here are made of cardboard, wood, and tin. A lot of the favela huts have no electricity, running water, or indoor toilets. Most of the people in these homes sleep in hammocks. These beds hang above the ground and are cool in hot weather. They don't cost much to buy and don't take up much space.

In São Paulo, it's not unusual to see shacks made of cardboard, wood, and tin located near modern high-rise apartments.

Many of the children from the favelas don't go to school. They spend their days begging. Some don't have families and have nowhere to go at night. Finding food can be really tough.

Brazilians are crowded together in the cities. But in the country, they often live miles away from one another. In the pampas region, for example, a kid could leave the family farm and walk for two days without running into anybody else (except for a couple of cows).

Many people in the pampas region of southern Brazil live on isolated farms.

Will the Real Capital City Please Stand Up?

Imagine if Americans couldn't decide where their capital should be. New York? Washington? Chicago? That's what happened in Brazil. Early Portuguese settlers chose Salvador, a city in the north. Then explorers discovered gold in the south, and where there's gold, people follow. Soon the capital was moved to the southern city of Rio de Janeiro. But Rio sits on the coast, and many Brazilians wanted the capital of their big country to be in a central spot. So in 1960 the capital was changed again. This time it moved to Brasília in central Brazil. Everybody must have gotten tired of all that moving around, because the capital's still there.

Vendors at this market in the city of Salvador sell a variety of colorful fruits and vegetables that come from eastern Brazil's fertile soil. Many products grown by Brazilian farmers end up in your local grocery store.

Farm **Handy**

 When you have breakfast tomorrow morning, check out what everyone's drinking. There's a pretty good chance the adults' coffee and your hot chocolate came from Brazil. Did your father have a glass of o.j.? It may have come from Brazil, too!

Most of Brazil's farms belong to just a few very rich landowners. But many of the farmworkers earn less than $50 a month. (Workers in the United States can earn more than that in a single day.) Farms in the south and southeast grow much of the world's wheat, oranges, and coffee. Up north, the biggest crop is cocoa beans.

Some workers bring their families to live on the plantations. The kids go to school right on the farm. Workers who don't live on the plantations get up at sunrise and hop on a bus for a long ride to work. These people are called *boias frias* (which means "cold meal") because of the cold lunch they carry with them every day.

Did you have a hamburger for dinner last night? The beef in your burger might have come from a Brazilian cattle ranch. Some of the workers on Brazil's ranches are called gauchos, or cowboys. On the job, these men wear big hats, wide pants, and capes called ponchos. Gauchos herd their cows through the southern pampas.

Brazil's many different landscapes provide jobs for a variety of Brazilians, from **coffee pickers** (above) **to gauchos** (left).

Think about what you ate yesterday. How much of your food came from somebody's farm? Do you think any of it came from Brazil?

Talk to **Me!**

The first European settlers in Brazil came from Portugal, so Brazil's official language is Portuguese. However, Brazil has lots of people from other lands. They sometimes speak their languages, such as Japanese or Italian, at home. Native peoples of the Amazon have their own languages, too. Over the years, native, African, and European Brazilians have all contributed words from their languages to the country's vocabulary. That's why Portuguese spoken in Brazil is not always the same as Portuguese spoken way across the Atlantic Ocean in Portugal.

Similar, But Not the Same

The countries south of the United States make up **Latin America.** Most Latin Americans speak Spanish instead of Portuguese because Spain conquered these places a long time ago. Spain and Portugal are neighboring European countries, and their languages are very similar. Take a look:

English	Spanish	Portuguese
one	uno	um
two	dos	dois
three	tres	três
four	cuatro	quatro
five	cinco	cinco
six	seis	seis
seven	siete	sete
eight	ocho	oito
nine	nueve	nove
ten	diez	dez

Thousands of words from the languages of the Tupí-Guaraní Indians, for example, have become part of everyday Brazilian Portuguese. Did you know that the English words *jaguar* and *tapioca* come from the Tupí-Guaraní?

This sign says "we have coco gelado" in Portuguese. Coco gelado, a special Brazilian treat, is a cold coconut with the top cut off. You stick a straw inside and drink the coconut juice.

Planes, Trains, Cars, and **Canoes**

Because their country is so huge, Brazilians have a lot of ground to cover when they travel. In the countryside, workers often have to travel 50 miles or more every day to get to their jobs. The trip might be on the back of a truck or on board an old bus. Indians and other residents of the Amazon region usually climb into a canoe. Wealthy people often fly from one place to another.

In the cities, traffic is crazy because lots of people drive cars. Brazilians tend to get pretty wild when they're behind the wheel. They think of stoplights as nothing more than a suggestion. So look both ways—twice!—before you

Passenger boats (above) **and canoes** (left) **are two common forms of transportation in the Amazon region, where the river is the main highway.**

You'd better run fast if you want to get across **Avenida Presidente Vargas** (left) in **Rio de Janeiro. If you don't want to walk, you can try getting on one of the city's crowded trolleys** (below).

cross the street. You'll have to keep your head moving if you want to get across Avenida Presidente Vargas. This boulevard in Rio de Janeiro has 10 lanes for cars (and they still have traffic jams)!

Many of Brazil's larger cities have public transportation, such as buses and subway trains. But they're packed! In Rio people hang off the sides of the city's trolley cars if they want a ride.

A Mix of **Faiths**

The Portuguese brought the Roman Catholic religion to Brazil. Nine out of ten Brazilians are Catholics. Other Brazilians practice **Spiritualism,** which means they believe in spirits. For example, many Indian peoples believe in nature spirits and in the spirits of their ancestors. A lot of African Brazilian Spiritualists pray to gods and goddesses called *orixás*. Two of the main African Brazilian Spiritualist religions are called Candomblé and Umbanda.

Roman Catholic churches, like this one in Salvador (left), **can be found in almost every city and town in Brazil. A Candomblé priestess** (above) **dresses in white for special ceremonies.**

Brazilians often combine Catholicism and Spiritualism. Roman Catholics might celebrate holidays that honor orixás. Spiritualists might also go to Catholic churches.

Sink or Swim?

Many Catholic and Spiritualist Brazilians honor the African sea goddess Iêmanjá every year. Iêmanjá is especially important to people like fishers and their families, who depend on the water to make a living. On New Year's Eve, worshipers dress in white and go to a river or to the ocean to offer flowers to Iêmanjá. Because the goddess is considered to be very vain, people also bring her combs, mirrors, and makeup. If the gifts sink, it means Iêmanjá is pleased, and she will grant the giver's wishes. If the gifts float back to shore, her worshipers had better try a little harder!

These Samba musicians—known as *sambistas*—are performing at a musical revue in Rio de Janeiro.

Feel the **Beat**

Brazilians love music. They create, listen to, and dance to all kinds of rhythms. The *lambada*, for example, started in the Amazon region and was influenced by music from the islands in the Caribbean Sea. The samba mixes Latin American and African beats. Over the years, this style has mixed with other kinds of music, creating new forms like samba-reggae and samba-rock. One of the most popular kinds of Brazilian music is the *duplas sertanejas*, or country duos. (They aren't always sung by two people, though.) Just like a lot of country music in the United States, these songs tell tales of lost love, hard work, and small-town life.

Throughout Brazil people enjoy making and listening to music.

Make a Maraca

Brazilian kids love shaking maracas. These instruments are easy to use and to find. Brazilians often make maracas out of a dried vegetable called a gourd, which has rattling beans inside. You can make a maraca with stuff you've got lying around the house.

Fill one plastic egg (or a small cardboard box about the size of your hand) with 10 dried beans. Tightly tape the two halves of the egg together. If you're using a box, tape it shut. Decorate your maraca with magic markers, glitter, stickers, and anything else you can find. Then shake!

This woman in Rio is decked out to celebrate Carnaval. Some people work many months to create their elaborate costumes.

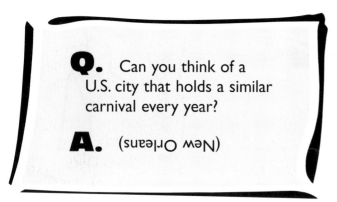

Q. Can you think of a U.S. city that holds a similar carnival every year?

A. (New Orleans)

Let's **Party!**

Everybody takes part in Carnaval (or Carnival), Brazil's greatest celebration. The week before the Roman Catholic season of Lent (which starts in February or March), schools and offices shut down completely. Even the smallest towns get ready for four straight days of dancing, music, parties, and parades. In the cities, people start working on their dazzling costumes and massive floats months before the big event. Everyone wants to be the biggest, the brightest, and the best when they march down the street through streams of confetti and wildly cheering crowds!

Every community celebrates Carnaval in its own way. In Rio musical groups called samba schools practice all year before they play in the parade. Each group wants to win the Carnaval champion prize.

In Salvador brightly lit floats carry musicians through jammed avenues as men, women, and kids cheer them on. And in Recife, the streets are filled with people dancing the *frevo*. The name for this dance comes from the Portuguese word *ferver*, which means "to boil." If you ever find yourself in the middle of thousands of people dancing to the beat of hundreds of drums, you'll know why it's considered so hot!

Parades, music, and brightly colored outfits mark Carnaval festivities. In Rio spectators can watch the parade from the Sambodromo, designed especially for Carnaval.

Any Excuse *Will Do*

Carnaval isn't Brazil's only celebration. In fact, most Brazilians will accept any excuse for a party! Many Brazilian kids say June is their favorite month because of the *festas juninhas*, or June festivals. These festivals celebrate several Catholic saints. Throughout the month, people hold barbecues, dances, and all-night bonfires. Children release hundreds of colorful balloons into the air and then watch as their parents light fireworks for them after dark.

Knot a Bonfim Bracelet

Every Brazilian city has its own celebrations throughout the year. During Salvador's Festival do Bonfim in January, people give thanks to Our Lord of Bonfim, a major saint. For good luck, thousands of people also exchange Bonfim ribbons. Why don't you and your friends do the same? Take one ribbon and tie it in knots around a friend's wrist. For each knot you tie, the wearer gets one wish. (Feel free to use lots of knots!) After a while the ribbon will wear out and fall off on its own (no fair pulling at it), and the wishes will come true. But you can't tie your own bracelet—the ribbon has to be a gift.

Brazilian Festivals

There are so many festas (festivals) in Brazil, it's hard to find a week without one! Here are a few of the more important national holidays.

January 1	New Year's Day
February (week before Lent)	Carnaval
March or April	Good Friday, a Catholic holiday on the Friday before Easter
May 1	Labor Day, celebrating the workers of Brazil
May or June	Corpus Christi, a Catholic holiday
June (all month)	Festas Juninhas
September 7	Independence Day
October 12	Nossa Senhora de Aparecida (honors Brazil's patron saint)
November 2	All Souls Day, a Catholic holiday
December 25	Christmas
December 31	New Year's Eve

In Brazil almost all celebrations involve dancing!

31

You Think Your
Exams Are Rough!

Brazilian kids go to primary school from the time they're 6 until they're 13 or 14. Every year students have to take a final exam. If they pass, they can move up to the next grade. But if they don't pass, they have to repeat the year. And guess what? School vacation lasts from January to March (remember, that's their summer).

School is free for everyone, but the level of education is very different depending on where you live. A child in the Amazon may go to a one-room school in a mud hut with only one teacher. In the countryside, the nearest high school might be 50 miles away. So a lot of kids in these places don't go to high school. They find work instead.

A young Brazilian pays attention in class.

In cities and towns, students in public schools have to buy their own uniforms and books. Some parents can't afford to send their children to school. Because so many kids don't go to school or don't finish their studies, one out of every five Brazilians can't read.

Children from wealthy families often go to private schools. Students in these schools take more classes and are in school longer each day. They may even have private lessons after school. Many wealthy kids go on to college after high school. To get into college, students have to pass a difficult exam.

A one-room schoolhouse in the Amazon region

Maybe Homework's Not So Bad

Many Brazilian grade-school children work when they aren't studying. Before or after school, city kids might have jobs selling food or newspapers in the street. To make sure these working kids get a chance to go to class, some schools teach one grade in the morning, starting at seven o'clock, another in the afternoon, and a third in the evening. The classes last about four or five hours.

GOOOAAAL!!!

Soccer, or *futebol,* is the most popular sport in Brazil. Many Brazilian kids start playing when they are very young.

Brazilians are absolutely, positively crazy about *futebol.* That's the Portuguese word for soccer. Except for private schools, most schools in Brazil don't teach sports. So kids squeeze in playtime wherever they can after school. Or they might watch a soccer game at home on TV.

Every major city has a futebol stadium. Rio's Maracanã Stadium can pack in 180,000 fans (some say 200,000 if nobody breathes). These fans go wild at every match. They paint themselves in their team colors, scream at every goal, and enjoy fireworks when the home team wins.

The international soccer competition is called the World Cup, and it takes place every four years. If you combine the Super Bowl, the World Series, and the NBA championship, you'll have some idea of how important the World Cup is to many countries. No one takes this event more seriously than Brazil. Its winning teams are treated like heroes, and the whole country mourns together when they lose.

Brazilians like other sports, too. Volleyball and basketball are popular. And because it's so hot in Brazil, lots of people head to the beach to go surfing, fishing, or boating.

Basketball is another popular sport among young Brazilians.

A Brazilian Hero

Pelé (Edson Arantes do Nascimento) was a poor teenager when he became a member of the Santos Futebol Clube, a soccer club in the state of São Paulo. At the time, he didn't even have a pair of shoes to play in. But in 1958, when he was 16, he helped Brazil win the World Cup. He led Brazil to two more wins before he retired, a national and world hero, in 1977. By that time, he had scored an unbelievable total of 1,281 goals. He is the only player to ever break 1,000.

Xuxa is a popular Brazilian TV star.

Shhh!
There's a Novela On!

Brazilians love to take advantage of their beautiful weather, so they spend a lot of time outside. But there's one thing that can always keep a Brazilian indoors—television! Kids all over the country love Maria da Graça Meneghel, but nobody calls her that. Xuxa, as she is known to Brazilians, has been the host of children's shows since 1983. She's had several programs, and they all feature music, dancing, games, and big, loud audiences filled with kids.

Meanwhile, Brazilian grown-ups are equally glued to the TV when the *novelas* come on. These TV soap operas tell the stories of people whose lives are so complicated they make U.S. soaps look boring. The novelas are on every night but Sunday, and people clear their schedules to watch their favorites. Not everyone in the countryside has a television, so the novelas give friends and neighbors a good excuse to get together after a hard day of work.

Brazilians aren't the only ones who love these shows. They're translated into Spanish so people in other Latin American countries can watch, too.

Brazilian TV offers a variety of programs for children and adults.

Check out these Internet sites for great information about TV, music, theater, sports—you name it—in Brazil. Try brazilonline.com or darwing.uoregon.edu/~sergiok/brasil .html#Culture.

Que rico! **(That means "how delicious" in Portuguese.) When** *feijoada* **is served with side dishes of rice, orange slices, and kale, it makes a delicious and colorful meal.**

Let's **Eat!**

Brazilians *love* to eat. The most popular dish is probably *feijoada*, a stew of black beans and smoked meats. The meats traditionally include the ears, tail, nose, and feet of a pig. The dish is served along with white rice, orange slices, a green vegetable called kale, and a dusting of *farofa*. Farofa is a toasted flour made from a starchy root called manioc.

As in any country, what you eat depends on where you eat. In Bahia, where African cooking is common, many recipes use coconut milk and spicy chili peppers. In the ranching country of the sertão, meat is a main ingredient. It's often served *churrasco* (barbecued) or *carne do sol* (sun-dried). There are over 2,500 kinds of fish in the Amazon, so you can guess what most people eat there! In Brazil's bigger towns and cities, you can stop at a food stand or open-air market for a bite. On the coast, it's fun to pick out your own coconut and watch the seller cut the top off. Then all you have to do is stick a straw inside and drink the juice!

Brazilian Fruit Salad

Try this refreshing salad made from fruits that grow in Brazil.

1 large banana
3 passion fruit
1 large orange

½ mango
1 star fruit

1 8-ounce can
pineapple chunks

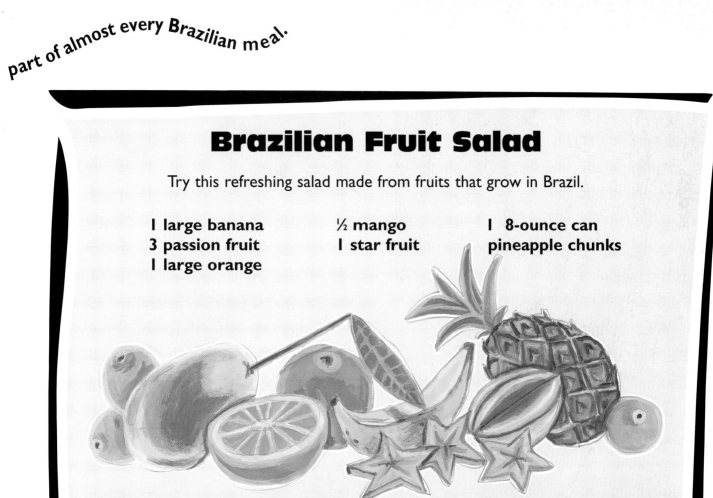

Ask an adult to help you prepare this fruit salad. If you can't find all the fruits, substitute strawberries, melons, and apples, which grow in Brazil, too. You'll need a large mixing bowl for the fruit, a knife, and a cutting board. Peel and slice the banana and orange into bite-sized pieces. Cut the star fruit into thin slices (the short way) so the pieces look like stars. Slice the passion fruit in half and spoon out the pulp in bite-sized pieces (it's okay to eat the seeds). Carefully slice the mango the long way until your knife reaches the fruit's hard inner pit. Continue to cut along the pit until you've sliced around the whole mango. Then pull the fruit apart. Scoop out one half with a spoon and slice it into bite-sized pieces. Then add the pineapple chunks. Stir the salad carefully to mix all the fruits. Serves four.

Going for a Visit

So you've been invited to have Saturday lunch with a Brazilian family? There are a few things you should know. First of all, get ready to be spoiled. Brazilians love entertaining and will do anything they can to make you feel welcome. If you're visiting people in the countryside, expect *lots* of welcomes. Families are often very large, with five, six, or more kids.

Grandparents usually live with their children or nearby, so they'll probably join you for lunch, too. And don't forget godparents. They tend to be very close to their godchildren and almost a part of the family. Brazilians are very affectionate no matter where they live. Don't be surprised if everybody hugs you or kisses you on both cheeks.

Before you arrive, you may want to stop at an outdoor market to pick up a gift. Maybe some tiny pineapples or a beautiful woven basket from the

The whole family gathers around the table at mealtime. If you are a guest, be prepared to eat!

All in the Family

Impress the whole family with your Portuguese when you go to a Brazilian lunch.

grandfather	*avô*	(ah-VOH)
grandmother	*avó*	(ah-VAW)
father	*þai*	(PY)
mother	*mãe*	(MY)
uncle	*tio*	(TEE-oo)
aunt	*tia*	(TEE-ah)
son	*filho*	(FEEL-yoo)
daughter	*filha*	(FEEL-yah)
brother	*irmão*	(eeh-MOWn)
sister	*irmã*	(eeh-MAHn)

Throughout Brazil grandparents live with their children and grandchildren.

Amazon? Don't worry if you're running a little late. Brazilians don't make dates for a specific time. If you're invited to come over around noon, that probably means anywhere from 12:30 to 1:30. And remember to show up hungry. Your hosts won't let you leave until you can't swallow one more bite of feijoada!

All over the country, artists use bright colors to decorate whatever crafts they're making. This tapestry above reflects Brazil's lush, tropical landscape.

Crafts That Are **Also Art**

Brazilians make crafts that match the materials and influences found in every part of this enormous land. In the southeastern state of Minas Gerais, for example, people weave gor-geous rugs with pictures of houses and churches like the ones in their region. You can put these rugs on the floor or hang them on the wall. The northeastern state of Ceará spe-cializes in multicolored, woven ham-

These two pots from
Santarém (right) **are examples
of Brazilian pottery. Children**
(below right) **relax in a locally
made hammock from the
state of Ceará.**

mocks with lace and crochet fringes.
Even people who have beds in their
homes often hang these from their
ceilings. In the fishing villages along
the coast, the women still weave
beautiful lace just like their grand-
mothers did. Brazilian lace-makers
are called *rendeiras.*

The most popular craft in Brazil is
pottery. Just like the other arts, the
style depends on where the craft is
made. In the southeast, yellow or
gray pieces reflect the color of that
area's clay. Similarly, the reddish
clay of the northeast produces red
pottery.

The giant leaves of the *Victoria amazonica* water lily

Glossary

drought: A long period of dry weather due to lack of rain or snow.

equator: The line that circles a globe's middle section halfway between the North Pole and the South Pole.

Latin America: The parts of the Americas south of the United States that were settled by Spaniards and that in modern times are ruled by their descendants. Latin America also includes Brazil.

martial arts: Several types of combat and self-defense, such as judo and karate, that are practiced both as an art form and as a sport.

Northern Hemisphere: The half of the earth's surface that lies to the north of the equator.

river basin: An area of land drained by a river and the smaller waterways that flow into it.

Southern Hemisphere: The half of the earth's surface that lies to the south of the equator.

species: Living things that share certain features and a common scientific name. Members of the same species can mate or breed to create offspring.

Spiritualism: A religious movement whose followers believe in and pray to spirits. The spirits may represent the ancestors of living people, common human personalities, forces of nature, or animals.

tropical rain forest: A dense, green forest that receives large amounts of rain every year. These forests lie in the hot regions of the world near the equator.

This furry creature is a three-toed sloth, one of the many animals that inhabits the Amazon rain forest.

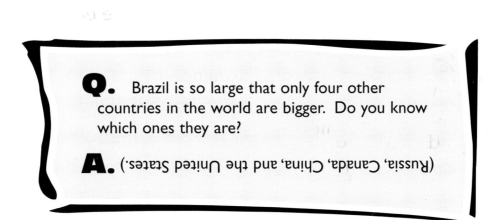

Q. Brazil is so large that only four other countries in the world are bigger. Do you know which ones they are?

A. (Russia, Canada, China, and the United States.)

Pronunciation Guide*

acarajé	ah-kah-rah-ZHAY
Bahia	bah-EE-uh
berimbau	beh-ree^n-BOW
boias frias	BOH-ahs FREE-ahs
Brasília	brah-ZEEL-yuh
caboclos	kah-BOHK-loos
Cabral, Pedro Alvares	kah-BROW, PEH-droo ow-VAH-rees
cafusos	kah-FOO-soos
capoeira	kah-PWAY-rah
carne do sol	KAH-nee doo SOH(W)
churrasco	shoo-HAHS-koo
coco gelado	KOH-koo zheh-LAH-doo
duplas sertanejas	DOO-plahs sehr-tah-NEH-zhahs
farofa	fah-HOH-fah
favela	fah-VAY-lah
feijoada	fay-ZHWAH-dah
festas juninhas	FAYS-tahs zhoo-NEE^n-yahs
frevo	FREH-voo
gaucho	GOW-shoo
Iêmanjá	yay-mah^n-SHAH
Iguaçu	ee-gwah-SOO
novela	noh-VAY-lah
orixás	oh-ree-SHAHS
Pantanal	pahn-tah-NOW
Pelé	peh-LAY
Rio de Janeiro	HEE-oo dee zhah-NAY-roo
São Francisco	SOW^n frahn-SEES-koo
São Paulo	SOW^n POW-loo
sertão	seh-TOW^n

*Translations are approximate.

Further Reading

Ashford, Moyra. *Brazil*. Austin: Steck-Vaughn, 1991.

Bender, Evelyn. *Brazil*. New York: Chelsea House Publishers, 1990.

Benson, Kathleen and Jim Haskins. *Count Your Way through Brazil*. Minneapolis: Carolrhoda Books, Inc., 1996.

Brazil in Pictures. Minneapolis: Lerner Publications Company, 1997.

Jacobsen, Karen. *Brazil*. Chicago: Children's Press, 1989.

Kent, Deborah. *Rio de Janeiro*. Danbury, CT: Children's Press, 1996.

Lewington, Anna and Edward Parker. *Brazil*. New York: Thomson Learning, 1995.

Lewington, Anna and Edward Parker. *Antonio's Rain Forest*. Minneapolis: Carolrhoda Books, Inc., 1993.

Oldfield, Sara. *Rain Forests*. Minneapolis: Lerner Publications Company, 1996.

Papi, Liza. *Carnavalia!* New York: Rizzoli, 1994.

Parnell, Helga. *Cooking the South American Way*. Minneapolis: Lerner Publications Company, 1991.

Thomson, Ruth. *The Rainforest Indians*. Danbury, CT: Children's Press, 1996.

Waterlow, Julia. *Brazil*. New York: The Bookwright Press, 1992.

Metric Conversion Chart

WHEN YOU KNOW:	MULTIPLY BY:	TO FIND:
teaspoon	5.0	milliliters
tablespoon	15.0	milliliters
cup	0.24	liters
inches	2.54	centimeters
feet	0.3048	meters
miles	1.609	kilometers
square miles	2.59	square kilometers
degrees Fahrenheit	5/9 (after subtracting 32)	degrees Celsius

Index